THE LIFE & TIMES OF

Benito Mussolini

BY
Tom Stockdale

SIENA

This is a Siena book
Siena is an imprint of Parragon Book Service Ltd

This edition first published by
Parragon Book Service Ltd in 1996

Parragon Book Service Ltd
Unit 13–17 Avonbridge Trading Estate
Atlantic Road, Avonmouth
Bristol BS11 9QD

Produced by Magpie Books Ltd, London

Copyright © Parragon Book Service Ltd 1996

Illustrations courtesy of: Hulton Deutsch Collection;
Peter Newark's Military Pictures; Bridgeman Art Library

ISBN 0 75251 566 7

A copy of the British Library Cataloguing in Publication
Data is available from the British Library.

Typeset by Whitelaw & Palmer Ltd, Glasgow

From the dizzy heights of the Roman Empire at the peak of its power, Italy had suffered from confusion and invasion: the dissolution of that empire, the Gothic onslaught and Charlemagne's supremacy, the static Middle Ages, the independent city states, attacks by other European countries, culminating in the final unification, more in name than in fact, in 1870. The people greeted their new status with a combination of expectation and continued independence, for many areas were as isolated under the new monarchy as they had been before it. Italy's poor economic base, and a political system controlled by the liberal upper-middle classes brought small reward to the hopes of Great Power status and empire which other European countries had taken on, despite the rapid and expanding industrialization of the north of the country.

From its beginnings in 1892, the Italian Socialist Party (PSI) made rapid advances in both the newly industrialized and traditional rural areas; meanwhile, Catholicism reacted to the godless age by politicizing with its own powerful trades unions. The dominant Ialian politician of the early twentieth century, the liberal Giovanni Giolitti, was forced to deal with increasing unrest in a country where pride was a vital and unstable currency.

Mussolini

A LION IS BORN

This was the Italy which greeted the son born to Alessandro and Rosa Mussolini on 29 July 1883, in Varnano del Costa, near Predappio, in the region of Romagna. 'The sun had just entered the constellation of Leo,' he would later write, with obvious pride. His blacksmith father was a self-educated socialist who wrote for several journals and squandered most of his earnings on his mistress. Named after three left wing revolutionaries, Benito Amilcare Andrea Mussolini grew up in an atmosphere of radical discussion and little respect for women. His mother, a schoolteacher, kept the family alive, and, although they were poor, there were always books in the two-room cottage for Benito and his brother Arnaldo to read.

Benito's official education was disjointed due to his aggressive character and unruly behaviour. At nine years of age he was sent away to a strict religious school, as his local school could not control him. During his second year there he was expelled after a stabbing incident. He was accepted at a more lenient establishment, where, despite repeated acts of bullying and consequent admonishment, he was allowed to complete his education. He left in 1901, aged eighteen, with a teaching diploma.

He had developed into an impressive figure,

short and powerful, with large, dark eyes. His dress was bohemian and his manner brutish, but his voice was deep and memorable. He took a temporary post at a school, and was already calling himself a socialist when, in 1902, the job came to an end and he went to Switzerland, either to satisfy an urge to travel, or to escape debts and vengeful husbands. He had followed his father's example in his dealings with women and had continued his sex education among the whores at a brothel close to his school. He seemed to delight in harsh descriptions of his liaisons, whether falling upon a prostitute or stabbing a mistress with a penknife, and he would never be without access to an outlet for his sexual demands. Women 'prefer brutality in a man to courtesy,' he said.

Once in Switzerland, he found himself unsuited to work on a building site, and was

Mussolini in 1904

soon arrested for vagrancy, though he was not held for long. Through a variety of short-term jobs he managed to survive. He started to write pieces for a socialist newspaper, and to make speeches calling for abolition and violent revolution, which marked him down as a radical. A voracious reader – although his learning was not of any depth – he picked out those elements he liked from the works of Marx, Nietzsche, Kant, the French syndicalist Georges Sorel, and others, and the combination of their philosophies and his journalistic leanings gave him an erratic, anarchistic way with language which became apparent in his aggressive speeches. He was arrested several times for trying to cause unrest and handed back to the Italian authorities, but he returned to Switzerland to avoid conscription in an army he was politically opposed to. Mussolini spent the next couple of years travelling around Central

Europe, preaching socialism and atheism, and gathering a reputation as a troublemaker.

In 1904 he returned to Italy and gave in to eighteen months' conscription. During his military service his mother died at the age of forty-six and his father was obliged to move from the cottage, which belonged to the school at which his wife had taught. Mussolini joined Alessandro after a year's teaching during which he contracted syphilis from a married woman. It became difficult for him to obtain other teaching posts, and he began to write for and edit a socialist journal. He was arrested during an agricultural strike, and his published advocacy of violent protest meant that his reputation grew in his local area. A further seven months in Austria brought more arrests, and the fathering of a son, while editions of the paper he wrote for were confiscated several times due to his aggressive and libellous style. Upon his expulsion from that country he picked up the editorship of a four-page weekly magazine in Forlì, called *La Lotta di Classe* (*The Class Struggle*) and spent the next two years calling for Marxist revolution, religious intolerance and military insubordination.

Mussolini set up house in Forlì with Rachele Guidi, the daughter of his father's mistress, in 1910, but it did nothing to make him want to settle down. Rachele was soon pregnant; she was to give birth to a second child before their marriage in 1915. Mussolini's career brought them little security, though his growing awareness of popular taste allowed him to write a serialized novel for the paper he had worked on in Austria. At the annual Socialist Party conference in 1910 he became angry at the absence of revolutionary consensus, and in 1911 he left the party, hoping to form a more radical one. His cause was assisted by Italy's invasion of Libya, and he was arrested after organizing a violent protest against it. A five-month prison sentence carried his reputation outside the Romagna – although there is no escaping the irony of the situation, considering his later imperialist ambitions. On his release, he realigned his small group with the Socialists, and at the next conference won both support and a place on the directorate.

Mussolini's increasing prestige helped him to the editorship of the socialist national daily paper *Avanti!* From 1912 to 1914 he used this as a base for attacks against the government, helping the Socialists to win 53 seats at the elections of 1913, although his own candidacy failed, and he doubled the paper's readership with his sloganizing and his angry editorials. He began a long relationship with

Margherita Sarfatti, who was to write his first official biography, and fathered another child by a different woman. When the First World War broke out in 1914 he stood foursquare with the party line that Italy must remain neutral. However, he soon become uncomfortable with this position, seeing the war as a bourgeois conflict from which the socialist revolution should arise. In October of that year he made public his change of mind and resigned as editor of *Avanti*!

It was now that Mussolini's beliefs moved on from those of his fellow socialists. He was partly forced into changing by having to defend his new position, as well as by the suspicion among his former colleagues that his founding of a new paper only two weeks after his resignation, with funding from French capitalism, implied more forethought than he was admitting to. Ownership of *Il Popolo d'Italia* soon taught him the social advantages of financial backing, and he found a political standpoint which would keep industrialists happy, while at the same time appealing to a mass readership. His new pro-war stance moved quickly from a call simply for a liberating war, to a war of territorial gain, and the quotes which were part of the paper's masthead signified Mussolini's direction: Auguste Blanqui's 'Who has iron has bread', and Napoleon's 'Revolution is an idea which has found bayonets'.

King Vittorio Emanuele III brought Italy into the war against Germany and Austria–Hungary in April 1915, despite the opposition of the majority of the Parliament. Mussolini was conscripted in September, and spent a relatively uneventful two years in uniform – though he later told stories of throwing back live grenades to the enemy –

until he was invalided out of the army in 1917
with wounds received during a training
exercise. He returned to his newspaper, now
a convinced anti-socialist as well as an anti-
capitalist.

After the end of the war in 1918, he showed
himself an acute reader of the public mood by
acting upon the disorientation of the people,
attracting the attention of returning soldiers,
nationalists and the poor, with anti-capitalist
headlines, while appealing to capitalists with
anti-socialist slogans. It was his ability to
perform for two disparate groups at the same
time which gave him support across the
political board, and on 23 March 1919 he
gathered a hundred or so people together to
form the party which would be the rallying
point for these elements: the Fascio di
Combattimento or Combat Group. In later
years the prestige of having been one of the

original group members was enough for thousands to claim their presence at the meeting.

FROM LEADER TO DICTATOR

Less than a month after the formation of the Fascist Party, the destruction of the offices of *Avanti!* gave notice that Mussolini's tactics included the use of violence against those the party saw as opposition. The disaffected soldiers were an ideal force to use for such bullying tactics, and although violence had been shown to be useful as a part of the Italian democratic system, the organization of Mussolini's *squadristi*, dressed in their black shirts and attracting converts by the simple fact of winning their battles, and mobilized by the headlines of the *Popolo d'Italia*, showed an authority which a disorganized country found appealing. The beatings, acts of vandalism and dosing of members of opposing groups with liberal quantities of castor oil were made to sound necessary by Mussolini's writing and speeches against the disruption of the post-war economy. He found backing from industrialists, as Fascist successes drew support away from trade unions in the towns, slowing down the rate of strikes, while the independent rural groups, with their leaders or *ras* adding their gangster style to the unruly ex-military element of the Fascists, gained in numbers. For the elections of 1921, the Fascists made an alliance with the Liberals and gained thirty-five seats, about 7 per cent, at the expense of 100 lives lost during violent electioneering. The Liberals put up with these tactics as an alternative to socialism gaining power, and only saw their mistake once Mussolini had got into Parliament and started to vote with the opposition.

Mussolini's greatest opportunistic moment came in August 1922, when a general strike was called by the weakening socialists; if the government would not prevent the strikes, he declared, his Fascists would. He seized upon the inter-party arguments which had been responsible for several short-lived governments, and threatened to use his armed forces in defence of peace; in other words, a legal version of the coup which he had already been discussing with some of his leaders. The 'March on Rome' became part of Fascist legend, although most of the marching was done in celebration of a *fait accompli*. On 28 October, the King refused to sign a decree for the mobilization of the army against the Fascists, perhaps because he

Mussolini in National Militia uniform, 1923

believed the estimates given by Mussolini of 300,000 armed men ready to march on the capital (a more accurate figure was 30,000). By now, the other parties were all interested in a coalition with the Fascists, as they were the vital young force in politics. Mussolini was offered a place in the next government, but he refused to join an administration which he did not lead. The next day, his bluff paid off and he was offered the position of Prime Minister; at the age of thirty-nine, he was the youngest Italian ever to accept it. He had used a combination of violence, cunning and charisma to lead a minor party with no set policies into power, just three and a half years after it had been formed.

The Italian electorate welcomed a leader who promised an end to the strikes and disruption of the recent past, and they loved the pomp of the rallies which Mussolini organized. His

Fascist poster

voice came into its own in speeches which combined pantomime and tabloid headlines, and the government he formed ran across the political spectrum, which surprised his detractors. His policies called for a combination of nationalization, authority and economic stability, and whatever his private desires were at this time, commentators at home and abroad were impressed by his stated plan to regenerate Italy. The combination of a parliament of factions whose members hoped to use Mussolini to keep their opponents out of power, and a populace who hoped that at last here was someone who could make an omelette out of the eggs he broke, meant that he had a couple of years in which to reinforce his position, and so ensure that he could not be voted out of power.

He made the *squadristi* into a National Guard, which gave him the benefits of a private army rewarded at the states's expense. Official positions were gradually filled by Fascist Party members, thus setting up a system of patronage for dutiful members, as well as making the party the only avenue by which anyone could rise in local government. In addition, he changed the electoral law so that the leading party in an election was automatically granted two-thirds of the seats in Parliament. As a result, in the 1924 elections blatant vote-rigging by the Fascists and the usual violence virtually guaranteed them 374 seats out of 535. Within the new Parliament, however, there were still a fair number of critics of Mussolini and his dicatorial style. One of the most outspoken of these, Giacomo Matteotti suddenly disappeared in June, and was found three days later. He had been stabbed to death. Although Mussolini could not officially be linked with the incident, it was clear that a vocal opponent had been eliminated, and it is known that the orders for the murder came from his senior lieutenants. Several of the democratic factions walked out of Parliament, but the remainder were not united enough to force Mussolini's hand; indeed, they still considered him to be useful to their plans for gaining power. For a time it was thought that he might still be forced to resign, until a group of his officers persuaded him not to bow to the opposition, but to eliminate it. So, in January 1925, Mussolini issued a public statement in which he assumed accountability for all that had occurred, and made it his responsibility to put the country to rights under his personal and absolute dictatorship. His majority in the pro-Fascist remainder of Parliament gave the decision its official backing.

Throughout the time that he had been moving towards the dictatorship, Mussolini had been making sure of the support of the

Fascists gather to hear Mussolini

people of Italy. Notwithstanding the outrages of his militia, his personal image was presented as that of a superman. As a reformer he was putting social changes and public works into effect, organizing the building of roads and planning new cities, avenues and cultural centres to make Italy the envy of the world. There were definite advances made in these areas, as there were in industrial relations and the stabilization of the economy. But, as Mussolini had learned a long time before, it was just as good to announce great works as to perform them. He was very aware of the power of the media, and the controls which he put upon the newspapers and journals which had been spared the ravages of the *squadristi* guaranteed that only good news would make its way into the consciousness of the masses.

He would pore over all the national and international press, dictating to editors when he could, putting pressure on others by the threat of confiscation. Foreign journalists were soon aware how uncomfortable they could be made if they wrote unfavourable articles, with the result that the world at large soon had a distorted picture of the new Italy. In the end, the success of this mass censorship was to become a problem for Mussolini himself, although he did not recognize it as such, for the combination of twisted news reports and the inevitable cloud of personal flattery which surrounded him made him believe the distorted image of himself and his successes which he had planned for outsiders. The fact that a favourable report could bring reward made a mockery of the economic and industrial figures as they appeared in the press or were presented in Parliament, and Mussolini would find to his cost the uselessness of inflated figures when the armaments that they apparently indicated could not be supplied.

IL DUCE

For the moment, the cult of *Il Duce* (The Leader) raged around the country. He was compared with Napoleon, Cromwell and Alexander the Great; he had the wisdom of the Greeks and the cunning of Machiavelli. His picture was in every house, his slogans were daubed on to walls. Of course, for every Caesar there is an assassin, and the four attempts on Mussolini's life in 1925-6 were turned into excuses for greater personal power. These bungled attacks were given a great deal of publicity in order to gather

The sportsman

sympathy for Il Duce, while the fourth attempt was the signal for his abolition of all political parties other than the Fascist Party. The death penalty was instated for anyone even planning to kill the leader, although, naturally, it was not necessary to be guilty of an offence to receive a visit from a unit of the secret police.

In fact, Mussolini's health was not particularly good, even though assassins' bullets might not have found their target. He loved to give the image of a man at home in the outdoors. Photographs often showed him running, sometimes bare to the waist. He liked to discuss his love of riding, boxing and fencing, and the theatricality of a personal appearance was sometimes heightened by his swapping places with one of his motorcycle outriders. The reality did not fit this healthy image. One result of his sexual athleticism was his long-term treatment for venereal disease, although blood samples sent to England were reported as clean. In 1925, after a collapse, he was diagnosed as having a gastro-duodenal ulcer, and was out of the public eye for a month. He was put on a strict diet, and from then on preferred to eat alone rather than make a weakness public. He had periodic repercussions of his illness, and lived mostly on milk and fruit, but continued in his impression of robust good health.

Between 1926 and 1930, Mussolini cemented his position in the country and increased state control in almost every sphere. The theory of the Corporate State, one in which all of industry is absorbed in the state, was one of the ideas which caused much interest around Europe, which was already involved in the alternatives of the market economy of the West, and Soviet collectivism. The Corporate

State would, it was said, bring an end to industrial strife by the joining together of workers and owners in their desire to serve the state, and would make the country completely self-sufficient. Mussolini called upon his cabinet only at irregular intervals, since he took sole responsibility for many of the departments of state; the various officials were there simply to carry out his decrees, and none of them lasted for any length of time, for it seemed that Il Duce was wary of anyone else taking control of anything. As a result, few men of any real ability came to prominence under him.

He saw very little of his family, living most of the time in hotels. Of the five children from his marriage, born between 1910 and 1929, only the oldest, Edda, was close to him, although the family was held up as a model for the rest of the country. His affair with

Mussolini with his family

Margherita Sarfatti was constant among many short term extramarital relationships, until 1930, when Rachele forced an end to the liaison. In 1936, aged fifty-three, Mussolini began the other great love affair of his life with Clara Petacci, a woman less than half his age, whose husband Mussolini exiled to Japan.

Il Duce was not a man given to keeping company and preferred to be seen as a workaholic, dealing personally with the smallest details of the running of the country. His impulsive nature led him to take a different mood at a moment's notice, a trait which was said to be a sign of his genius, for he loved to make unexpected decisions and wanted always to be seen as leading, rather than following advice. Meanwhile, the non-reporting of failures and the massaging of statistics made his infallibility seem a fact. The picture he attempted to give was of an Italy succeeding naturally to the glories of the Roman Empire, whose *fasces*, (bundles of rods surrounding an axe), carried by the lictors of ancient Rome, had been taken up by Mussolini as a symbol of Italian strength and unity.

Mussolini wanted the world to see Italy as continuing the cultural traditions for which it was rightly known. He set up various artistic, scientific and academic establishments, trying to attract talented individuals each of whom would swear an oath of allegiance to fascism before receiving a generous grant. There was an attempt to make Shakespeare out to have been Italian, and it was officially stated that the discoveries of Einstein were not original. It was difficult for Mussolini, however, to bend the imaginations of artists to the interests of the state, and many plays and films were

Fascist boys parade

banned or censored to protect the Fascist ideal.

By 1930, he was confident that the country was moulding itself to the Fascist image. On 11 February 1929 he had signed the Lateran Accord with the Roman Catholic Church after three years of secret talks, which, among other things, recognized the independent sovereignty of the Holy See in the Vatican City state, in return for the Church's recognition of the secular state. This ended 60 years of hostility between the two, and brought conservative and Catholic acceptance of Mussolini's government.

Mussolini had set up a system of education designed to place the 'continuous revolution' that was fascism uppermost in the mind of every child, and which saw four-year-olds in Fascist uniform and eight-year-olds drilling with scale models of army rifles. His economic policy was beginning to give the population the trappings of prosperity, while continuing the profitability of the capitalists. It has been said that if Mussolini had been as successful with his foreign policy as he was with his domestic agenda, his Italy would still be here today. However, it was this vital area of foreign relations which exposed Italy's desperate need for stable, honest growth, and which transformed a successful dictator into an overreaching megalomaniac.

A WORLD POWER

From his earliest propaganda speeches, Mussolini had used the imagery of revolution and violence, for he was a skilled speechmaker and knew the power of martial analogy and vocabulary. On his accession to power, he infused his plans for reform with the language of the battlefield. The economic revival was the battle of the lira, the drive to grow wheat was the battle for wheat, the plan to build a country of warriors was the battle for births – there was nothing that could not be fought and beaten. From 1930, the

31

metaphors took on a more aggressive realism as he came to believe that a country with the regained greatness of Italy needed an empire for its prestige and profit, despite the fact that the other European powers were finding that many of their colonies were economic burdens, rather than benefits.

Mussolini's entry into the area of foreign policy was more of an extension of propaganda than an attempt at diplomacy. Any international congress was an occasion for him to be seen on an equal footing with other heads of state, and his mere presence at such occasions was an event celebrating his powers of statesmanship, although the other nations considered his dramatic entrances and ill-timed comments to be of less help than was apparent from the rapturous reports which the carefully briefed Italian press carried home. Although on the surface Mussolini insisted on Italy's friendly relations with the rest of Europe, there were flurries of aggrandisement during the 1920s; among them the invasion of Corfu in 1923, which the British and French forced to be abandoned, and the establishment of a protectorate over Albania in 1926, which the League of Nations, not wishing to upset a regime which was helping to keep socialism at bay, agreed to acknowledge.

In addition, Mussolini was secretly trying to unsettle the balance of power in Europe, interfering in French areas of interest in the Balkans and sending arms and money to various revolutionary groups. He had done the same with radicals in Austria, keeping alive hopes of gaining border areas which he thought Italy should have been granted after the First World War. Money was also sent to assist the growing Nazi Party in Germany,

Arrival in Genoa

where Mussolini considered that a sympathetic right-wing leadership would help him in his greed for European soil. Other European leaders wanted his assistance in their attempts to keep the lid on the bubbling pot of socialism, and his authoritarian success was admired: Winston Churchill told him, 'If I were Italian, I am sure that I would have been with you from beginning to end in your victorious struggle.'

In Africa, the Libyan rebel resistance, which had been continuing since the days when Mussolini had spoken out against its invasion in Italy, had been crushed; he was also waiting for an opportunity to take control of Abyssinia (Ethiopia). There had been an Italian plan to invade the country since 1925, though the two countries signed a treaty of friendship in 1928. By the time Mussolini's speeches had become blatantly and belligerently militaristic, the armed forces had been built up, and in October 1935 a large Italian invasion force attacked Abyssinia after a minor incident which Mussolini characterized as Abyssinian aggression. The League of Nations imposed economic sanctions against Italy, but did not include oil amongst them. By May 1936 Italy had a new colony, and Mussolini announced a new pinnacle of fascism. The victory in Abyssinia was not, however, without enormous economic cost, as well as alienating the League of Nations. This in turn drew Italy closer to Germany under Adolf Hitler, its leader since 1933, as the only country willing to ally itself with an aggressive Italy.

Mussolini began his relationship with Hitler from a position of dominance. Fascism was the blueprint for Nazi Germany, and during his rise to power Hitler held the Italian

King Victor Emmanuel and Mussolini

dictator in awe. The real power in early-1930s Europe lay with Britain and France, and Mussolini wanted to squeeze as many concessions out of those two countries as possible. The two fascist leaders met for the first time in Venice during 1934, after which Mussolini described Hitler as 'a clown'. Six weeks later, however, in July, the 'clown' organized the assassination of Engelbert Dolfuss, the Austrian Chancellor, and the ensung Nazi-backed coup posed a real threat to Italy's Austrian border. Mussolini mobilized his border troops, forcing Hitler to back down, and thus increased his prestige in Europe, but he could see that Germany's ambition was becoming a match for his own, and that a common ideology could only bring the two countries closer together. By October 1936, the two countries had formed the Rome–Berlin 'axis', the metaphor being coined by Mussolini himself.

In July 1936, only two months after the conquest of Abyssinia, the start of the Spanish Civil War between the rebel Nationalist forces and the Republican government gave Mussolini further opportunity to see the direction in which his future lay. Secret Italian aid to General Francisco Franco's Nationalist forces soon became overt, and Germany put its support behind a revolution which would continue to disturb the balance of power in Europe. In 1937, Mussolini accepted Hitler's invitation to visit Germany, during which he was treated to example after example of Nazi might. He carried back to Italy a copy of the Anti-Comintern Pact, by which Italy, Germany and Japan agreed to a containment of communism; he brought, too, the beginnings of an aping of Nazism, starting with the adoption of the goose step by the Italian military, and moving on to encompass laws against the Jews. When Hitler invaded Austria in March 1938, resuming the plan to which Mussolini had put a stop four years before, Il Duce simply sent his regards. He had hitched the chariot of Italian destiny to the tank of German ambition, and took no notice of popular feeling against the Nazi *Anschluss* in Austria.

In May 1938, Hitler made a return visit to Rome; he did not, however, tell Mussolini that his plans to invade Czechoslovakia were almost complete. The Führer had already decided not to trust his ally with the full extent of his ambition, and it was obvious to any observer that, despite Mussolini's claims of '8 million bayonets', the Italian arms machine was not up to scratch, and that Italy was useful more as a diversion for enemy forces than as an equal partner in an invasion. Mussolini had long had designs upon Czechoslovakia as an extension of Italian

The Hitler–Mussolini alliance, 1938

territory, but when German troops began massing for an attack he knew that he had been beaten to the punch. Having nothing to gain by simply looking on, he took advantage of a request by Britain's Prime Minister, Neville Chamberlain, to arrange a conciliatory meeting with Hitler. The meeting in Munich in September 1938 – at which there were no Czechoslovak representatives – ended up giving Hitler half of what he wanted. Once again Mussolini was seen as the peacemaker of Europe, and on his return to Rome he was greeted as the victor of a mighty campaign. Six months later, Hitler strode into the rest of Czechoslovakia without a word to Mussolini, who was hurt and embarrassed.

As a counter to Hitler's rudeness, Mussolini gave no notice when he invaded Albania in April 1939. Albania was already an Italian

Hitler dominates Mussolini, 1938

protectorate, and the country was barely able to mount a defence, but the sloppy annexation was presented as a smoothly run operation by an army which would soon be ready to overcome the might of the French. The Germans were piqued, but this did not hinder the signing of the 'Pact of Steel' in May, by which Italy and Germany formally agreed to mutual aid in the case of either of them becoming involved in a war. Though this meant that Italy was officially alienated from Britain and France, Mussolini was not expecting to have to fight those countries until his own forces had been properly rearmed. His plans gave 1943 as the earliest date at which Italian forces could be unleashed upon the rest of Europe, and Hitler let him think that he agreed to this timetable, not telling him of his own intention to invade Poland as soon as was practicable. In a repeat performance of the attack on Czechoslovakia, it was only German troop movements along the Polish border which gave the game away. On 1 September 1939 Germany declared war on and invaded Poland. Mussolini seemed to be caught in a situation whereby, in accordance with the Pact of Steel, he would be obliged to fight alongside Germany with a seriously underpowered force; at the same time, however, he was desperate to show the world Italy's destiny in action. He was temporarily let off the hook when Hitler asked him whether he needed any arms and supplies. On the advice of his military commanders he requested enormous amounts of both, and when Hitler asked when he would need them, gave the answer, 'Immediately'.

Italy was, therefore, given some breathing space, but Mussolini watched the speed of German advances into Poland with despair and envy. As Britain and France declared war on Germany (3 September), Mussolini began a continuous tirade against his commanders, while continuously changing his mind as to what he should do. He was determinedly non-neutral, yet apparently 'non-belligerent', but his main worry was that not only was Italy losing her prestige by non-involvement, but she was in danger of losing the easy pickings which Germany was already collecting. He saw Hitler as unbeatable, but wanted him to be held up by the Allies while Italy rearmed. One minute, the Germans were 'mere soldiers, not real warriors', the next, they had a 'fine martial spirit' and a 'heroic philosophy'.

In March 1940, the two leaders met at the Brenner Pass, where Hitler attacked Mussolini's pride by intimating that if Italy did not join the fight against the Allies she would be a second-class power. In the next month German troops successfully invaded Denmark and Norway, and in May advanced into Belgium, on their way towards France. Mussolini suddenly saw Hitler winning the war single-handedly, and so rejected a letter from Winston Churchill, who had succeeded Chamberlain as Prime Minister on 11 May, appealing to him to prevent the spilling of Italian and British blood. Il Duce reminded Churchill of the sanctions taken against Italy when she invaded Abyssinia, and declared that the Pact of Steel would be maintained with honour. In other words, he had seen the winning side and was keen to join it as soon as possible.

Despite the best advice of his generals, Mussolini announced that he wanted to enter the conflict the next month. It seemed that he feared that the war would soon be over, for he remarked to his Chief of the General Staff, Marshall Pietro Badoglio, 'Everything will be over by September and . . . I only need a few thousand dead so that I can sit at the peace conference as a man who has fought.' The Italian declaration of war against Britain and France was made on 10 June 1940. A day earlier Mussolini had announced it to the Italian people, in a speech which he must have been refining for years. It ended with the words, 'People of Italy, to arms! Show your courage, your tenacity and your worth.' It was rapturously received by the crowds who heard him.

MUSSOLINI AT WAR

The truth was that Mussolini did not have much of a force to mobilize. Much of the army's equipment was outdated, the navy had no aircraft carriers, the air force had only 1,000 aircraft – there were not even properly equipped field kitchens. Mussolini was not the head of the armed forces because of his aptitude for the job; he would far rather have been organizing new uniforms or lying in the arms of a mistress than tending to the complexities of a well-run army. Hitler commanded his own troops; Mussolini therefore wanted to lead his. He was still prepared to accept overestimates of Italian armed strength, and he was served by officers who still gave them. But while the use of false information was an advantage in controlling the population, it was dangerous stupidity to employ it in directing an army on a war footing.

The timing of the declaration of war was unfortunate in terms of Mussoloni's ambitions, since France, defeated and in part overrun, requested an armistice of the Germans before a move could be made. He resigned himself to several border skirmishes with the already defeated enemy, which were halted by a snowstorm.

There followed several weeks' inactivity, during which Mussolini looked around desperately for someone to attack. His offer to Hitler of support for an invasion of Britain was rejected, while the alternative of controlling the Mediterranean did not seem filled with the promise of glory. In the skirmishes which took place between the British and Italian navies, the minor British losses were described as '50 per cent of British naval potential'; meanwhile, Italy lost ten per cent of her slow-to-submerge submarines in the first three weeks of the war.

Mussolini demanded action in North Africa, where small British forces had already been on the offensive. He planned to overrun Egypt with the much greater Italian forces which had gathered in Libya. In fact the Italian advance was slow and short, and stopped moe than 50 miles from the first strong British defensive position in order to wait for supplies. The mere fact of an Italian advance, however, gave Mussolini immense pleasure, and he was able to give a positive report to Hitler at their next meeting. But once again Hitler neglected to tell Mussolini of his immediate plans, so that the German takeover of Romania on 7 October 1940 came as an unpleasant surprise. Mussolini again decided to play Germany at its own game – to 'pay Hitler back in his own coin', as he freely admitted. While continuing to rail against the slow-moving forces in Egypt, a strategic kingpin in the battle for control of the Suez Canal, he moved troops in Albania up to the Greek border. He claimed that these were precautionary movements against any British advance through Greece, but in fact the real point of his plan was to create a parallel war to Hitler's in western Europe. On 28 October an impossible ultimatum was presented to the Greeks and rejected by them, and the Italians moved across the border. Hitler was informed too late to take any action, and Mussolini settled back to witness a speedy victory over weak opposition.

However, the Italian advance was so slow that Greece had time to mobilize, and the combination of mountainous terrain and the fact that they were fighting on home soil made the Greek forces more formidable than Mussolini had bargained for. In three weeks the Greeks beat off some of Italy's finest divisions and themselves began to advance into Albania. Mussolini blamed the incompetence of his officers. Hitler was disgusted, for an undefeated Greece was now likely to ally herself with Britain. Mussolini's commander for the campaign, Badoglio, resigned, but his successor did nothing to prevent further Greek success, despite orders that Italian soldiers were to die at their posts rather than give ground.

After Christmas, the Italian troops were reinforced for a counter-offensive. Mussolini was due for another meeting with Hitler, and was understandably nervous that he might receive a verbal beating for the failure of his army to overrun an inferior foe. The positions of the two leaders had turned about face during the few years that they had known each other. From now on, Hitler would be able to play upon Mussolini's weakness and pride, and so keep Italy in the minor role that he had always planned for her. The Italian troops failed to beat back the Greeks once more. In the event, the meeting with Hitler went better than Mussolini had feared, and he was given another chance to defeat the Greeks on his own.

A third offensive was launched in March 1941, and was another failure. In April, less than a month later, Italy's humiliation was complete as German divisions rolled into Yugoslavia and Greece, ultimately forcing the surrender of both countries, and driving out or capturing

British forces fighting in support of the Greeks. Italy was given no scraps from the territorial reorganization which followed, and Mussolini was shown to be at the head of a useless force. Worse things had already happened when a British advance into Libya, begun in December 1940, had proved successful. By the end of that year Italy was back to square one as far as an invasion of Egypt was concerned, and by the end of January 1941 the Libyan port of Tobruk had fallen to British and Dominion troops. A total of 130,000 Italians had been taken prisoner, and ten of its crack divisions put out of action. Mussolini was forced to accept a takeover of command by Lieutenant-General Erwin Rommel, who arrived with the German Afrikakorps in February.

The scale of these disasters could not be disguised by Mussolini's propaganda machine, and the Italian people, who had been less than jubilant over the alliance with Germany (and thousands of whom had been keener to join the fight to save Poland from the Nazis), were starting to feel the effects of economic isolation. Despite Mussolini's claims of self-sufficiency in food, supplies were short even by 1941. Food queues were long, the black market was flourishing, and there were often Fascist Party officials making a profit out of the suffering of the ordinary citizen. Mussolini's position as the sole figure in charge of his people's destiny made Italy's lack of military success attributable directly to him.

Late June 1941 saw the commencement of another dangerous diversion for Il Duce, as Germany abandoned her 'non-aggression' agreement with the Soviet Union, the Nazi–Soviet Pact of 23 August 1939, Mussolini was woken in the middle of the night to be informed that massive German

forces had attacked Russia, and was as angry
about the casual way in which he had been
treated as he was about the information which
Hitler had decided to share with him.
However, the prospect of extending the
Italian empire to the east was too tempting,
and he announced that 60,000 troops were to
be sent to join the new offensive, despite
German advice to concentrate his forces in
North Africa. Rommel's first manoeuvre had
by 26 April pushed the British back into
Egypt. By 5 May the British had overrun the
Italian forces in Abyssinia in less time than it
had taken Mussolini to annex the country just
five years earlier, and for the Axis it was
psychologically as well as strategically
important for the Allied oil transport route via
the Suez Canal to be put under pressure.
Mussolini decided, however, that his people
would be excited by the thought of fighting
on another front, not thinking of the

problems of leadership, manpower, arms and supplies which had let Italy down so badly already.

Mussolini's mental state was giving cause for concern, as his anti-German feeling rose to new heights. He talked of the need for defence during the war which would inevitably be joined between Italy and Germany, and a tour of the Eastern Front in August was made miserable by the obvious evidence of German might, and by monologues from Hitler lasting for up to two-and-a-half hours. The only highlight for him (and of course for the newspapers at home) was when he took the controls of Hitler's plane on the way back, flying being one thing he could do that Hitler could not. The Führer would have been even more nervous had he known that, after a serious training accident 18 years before, an instructor had been secretly hidden aboard the plane during the examination in which Mussolini made his first solo flight.

At first, Mussolini's decision to join the war on the Eastern Front seemed a good one, as the Soviets were pushed back. He determined to increase the number of Italian troops in Russia, although there were not enough arms and trucks for those already there, let alone warm clothing for the winter, since the Russians had been expected to crumble within weeks. He was assured, however, that the war was almost won. '200,000 soldiers in Russia will weigh more than 60,000 when finally we come to the peace conference,' he said. The difficulties of supply were beginning to cause enormous problems, however, as the Russian tactic of attacks followed by retreats, leaving devastated villages and poisoned water supplies behind them, forced the Axis troops to spread out over hundreds of miles.

A LION LAID LOW

The balance of the Second World War was dramatically altered on 7 December 1941 with the Japanese attack on Pearl Harbor. Mussolini was in full favour of Japan's entry into the war on the Axis side, and of the attack; he considered America to be racially and militarily weak, and he dismissed reports of her productive capacity as propaganda. Although he was disheartened by an Allied attack which relieved Tobruk at the end of the year, Rommel successfully counter-attacked (ignoring an order to halt from his nominal commander, Il Duce). As a result, Mussolini's spirits rose through the first few months of 1942, and he planned to be in the forefront of the charge to Suez. He had been promised Italian civilian domination of Egypt by Hitler, and wanted to make a victor's entry into Cairo on a white stallion.

The main Axis attack began in May. Mussolini was on tenterhooks, waiting for the moment after the danger had passed, but before the threat of it was over. He set off after the surrender of Tobruk on 29 June, but by the time he got there, the battle had become static at El Alamein. He spent three weeks at a safe 500 miles from the front line, hearing of nothing but Rommel, and pretending that he was there to inspect his troops. Then he returned to Rome, low in spirits and physically ill. He was diagnosed variously as suffering from amoebic dysentery, an ulcer and, by rumour, cancer and syphilis. One of his commanders called it 'a less commonplace disease. It's called humiliation.' He recovered through the summer at his retreat on the Adriatic, while his officials despaired at his poor health and his indecision. There began to be whispered talk of the search for a possible successor.

There was to be no upswing of the pendulum, whatever fighting talk Mussolini communicated through the summer of 1942, and as autumn closed in, the news from North Africa and Russia grew worse and worse. In October, the Allies forced the Axis to retreat at the second battle of El Alamein, leaving thousands of Italians to flee on foot. In November Allied forces, which now included Americans, landed in Morocco and Algeria, sweeping the Axis out of North Africa by May 1943, and providing a springboard for an invasion of Italy.

The Russians had withdrawn as far as Stalingrad, which the Germans and their allies attacked in September 1942, The Soviet forces resisted fiercely, fighting from street to street and house to house. Then the snows came sweeping across the straggling lines of Axis troops. Mussolini urged Hitler to come to a settlement with the Soviet Union so that their forces in Russia could be redirected to the Mediterranean, but the Führer was insistent in his belief that the war on the Eastern Front was his for the winning. In November massed Soviet armies counter-attacked at Stalingrad; in November they broke through German and Italian lines, leaving the survivors to walk or crawl back westward, or perish of cold and hunger: 115,000 Italians alone died on the march back to 'civilization'.

In Italy, Allied bombing of principal cities had intensified, and rationing was also beginning to have an effect on civilian morale, as the staple foods disappeared. Black market prices were up to five times the normal, and any food whose price was curbed would mysteriously disappear from the shelves. Many consumer items were simply unavailable to civilians in a climate where military production was not able to keep up with losses sustained in war.

The presence of the Americans in the war had a great psychological effect on the Italian people. There was a palpable collective movement towards opposition to the war, and there were disturbances which were met with violence from the security forces. Mussolini's propaganda machine was starting to crack, as more people got their information from Allied radio broadcasts – the disparity between them and the official programmes was obvious. Disgust grew at the wealthy

Fascist Party officials, at the political dabbling of Clara Petacci's family, at state lies and corruption, and, above all, at the man who had dragged Italy into the situation in the first place, Benito Mussolini.

Mussolini continued to involve himself with trivial decisions – indeed, they consumed ever more of his time – and at the beginning of 1943 he made major cabinet changes in an attempt to show his continuing control at the top. But his intuition had deserted him, and he shuffled his enemies and rejected his supporters seemingly at random. He sacked Count Galeazzo Ciano, husband of his daughter, Edda, as Foreign Minister, taking on the position himself. Another minister he appointed was resident in a mental institution at the time. The celebration of his sixtieth year was played down at his own command, as he tried to hide the advancing years that his

body and mind were showing only too
clearly.

The last Italian footholds in Africa had been
lost when Tunisia and Libya were overrun,
though Mussolini's continuing bouts of illness
seemed to prevent him appreciating the full
extent of the defeat; he had lost three stones
in weight since the summer before, and spent
a lot of his time even now playing with
newspaper headlines. The Russians were
preparing to move west again. In March 1943
there was the first strike in Italy since 1922,
which grew into a general strike that halted
many major war industries. And in April,
another meeting between Mussolini and
Hitler had the effect of persuading the latter
to prepare troops for an occupation of Italy,
so weak did Mussolini appear and so
despairing of the future of fascism. There
were already several German units 'training'

in Italy, and Mussolini was all too aware of their sinister potential.

At the beginning of June, the 'impregnable' island of Pantellaria, in the channel between Tunisia and Sicily, became the first piece of Italian soil to fall to the Allies, and on 9 July they landed in Sicily. King Vittorio Emanuele had already been working towards a plan to depose Il Duce without the monarchy suffering, and after he had had another ineffectual meeting with Hitler, Mussolini's commanders decided to remove him from power. During the meeting, word had come of a heavy bombing raid on Rome, which was a final psychological bastion to the Italians, who had always been sure of the safety of the capital's archaeological treasures, and the sanctity of the Vatican City. Several brave members of the Fascist Grand Council managed, though they were fearful of being arrested for treason, to get Mussolini to agree to a meeting of the Council.

On 24 July 1943, Mussolini opened the meeting with a rambling two-hour speech full of blame and vague plans, and Dino Grandi, a former Foreign Minister, who had left home that morning with a hand grenade and a newly written will, had to wait before rising to declare Mussolini's dictatorship immoral, and to put a resolution that the dictator should hand over his powers. After nine hours of debate, the vote was cast. Nineteen out of twenty-eight members of the Council voted with Grandi. The former Duce reacted almost as though nothing had happened. Next morning he was at his desk as usual. It was as though his mind had suffered an overload and he was stuck in a habitual pattern of behaviour. The Mussolini of old would have immediately had the nineteen

Mussolini fallen from power, July 1943

arrested, and though he talked about it, he did nothing. That afternoon he had an audience with the King, expecting to be able to overturn the decision of the Grand Council. The King told him instead that he was the most hated man in Italy, and that he was to be succeeded by Marshal Badoglio. Italy was no longer a dictatorship. The twenty-one years of Mussolini's rule were over.

The relief of the people of Italy could be heard that evening, and seen the next morning by the jettisoned pictures and statues of Il Duce lying in the streets. It seemed that during the night fascism had died. While Badoglio tried to set in motion a plea to the Allies to let Italy join the fight against Germany, Mussolini was taken via several police barracks to the island of Ponza, 60 miles almost due west of Naples, where he was to be given protection for his own safety.

He dictated a letter of good wishes to Badoglio and guaranteed his good behaviour. Ponza had been used up to then to exile enemies of fascism; now its leader was to taste the bare comforts of his own treatment amongst several of these political prisoners. After ten days he was moved to the bleak island of La Maddalena, off the northern coast of Sardinia, as it was thought that the Germans might make a rescue attempt in order to set up a new fascist government. From there, after three further weeks, he was taken back to the mainland, to a ski hotel at Gran Sasso in the Appennine mountains. 'The highest prison in the world', he called it.

He spent his time comparing his betrayal with those of Christ and Napoleon, and in consideration of the possible judgement that history would pass upon him, seeming to take little notice of the air raids which were battering his people and the German troops who had taken over his country. Meanwhile the Allies, having crossed to mainland Italy from Sicily, started to move up from the far south. On 8 September, US General Dwight D. Eisenhower, Supreme Allied Commander in the Mediterranean theatre, forced Badoglio's hand by announcing Italy's surrender, although the Cabinet was still debating the latest Allied ultimatum. Badoglio confirmed the decision nearly two hours later. Germany reacted with speed, taking over Italian positions in northern and cental Italy, while the King and the government escaped to Brindisi and the protection of the Allies.

On 12 September 1943, just over two weeks after his arrival at Gran Sasso, Mussolini was dramatically rescued by SS Lieutenant-Colonel Otto Skorzeny, who had been charged with the task of finding the hiding

Mussolini rescued by Skorzeny

place. In a mission straight out of fiction, eight gliders crash-landed near the hotel. Skorzeny had brought with his team an Italian general, whose orders confused Mussolini's guards effectively enough for the mission to be accomplished without a shot being fired. The ex-dictator was taken out in a tiny Fieseler-Storch spotter plane, which just managed to take off from the short slope which ran down to a precipice. He showed all the signs of physical and mental exhaustion, but once at Hitler's headquarters at Rastenburg, he was lectured and bullied into proclaiming himself the leader of an Italian Social Republic, though this was nothing more than an official mouthpiece for the controlling German forces in the area not under Allied control.

The capital of the new state was the town of Salò, near Lake Garda in the north of Italy.

Mussolini was installed there with his family, while Clara Petacci was also rescued and moved nearby on Hitler's orders. The two Fascist leaders described themselves as each other's only friends, but Hitler also needed Mussolini's symbolic leadership of fascism to support the German presence in Italy. In addition, although Mussolini had no hand in the actual administration of his new state, his name lent legitimacy to the acts of brutalism which the Germans carried out against the population, forcing men and boys to join the revived Militia and rounding up Jewish communities in accordance with Nazi practice.

Mussolini's fall from power had brought the anti-Fascists in to the open, and the reinstatement of fascism from Salò caused the outbreak of a civil war between the two factions which was to run in counterpoint to

The Allied advance through Italy

the main battle for Italy between the Axis and the Allies. Fascist authority was stamped upon the population in January 1944 by the trial and execution of five of the members of the Grand Council who had voted against Il Duce in June, including Ciano, Mussolini's son-in-law. Mussolini, whose mood swings were continual, seemed not to care. 'He thinks only of history,' said one of his ministers, 'and how he will appear in it.'

In Italy as a whole, the northward advance of the Allies allowed democratic government to resume in its wake, with power apportioned between the various political groups. Foodstuffs were in very short supply, black marketeering was rife, and townspeople were often forced to walk into the countryside to scavenge for food – in many towns the cat population virtually disappeared. Partisan groups grew in number, hiding in the hills in between strikes on German troops; in some areas Nazi retaliation was to kill ten civilians for every dead German. The battle for Naples had largely been won by the population of the city itself, and the Germans ransacked it before they left, planting bombs, some of which were timed to go off weeks later.

Through the winter of 1943-4 the Allies were entrenched along a line south of Bologna, and during the winter the partisan units in the German-occupied areas grew in strength and numbers under the direction of the Committee of National Liberation for Northern Italy. The spring of 1944 saw the continuation of the Allied advance, and Rome fell in June. During that time, Mussolini made several trips to see Hitler in Germany; one of them, in July, was on the day of the unsuccessful attempt to assassinate the Führer. Mussolini was almost relieved to

The strung-up bodies of Mussolini and
Clara Petacci

see the evidence of opposition to the leader who had him under his control.

By the beginning of 1945, it was clear that, as Hitler said, 'Whether it is we or the English who take the Italians' trousers, it comes to the same thing.' Mussolini kept up his talk of fighting 'to the last Italian', but in March he tried to negotiate a surrender to the Allies through the Archbishop of Milan. The unconditional terms demanded of him were, even at this late stage, too high a price, he decided. On 25 April the Committee of National Liberation declared the death penalty for all Fascist leaders, and Mussolini learned that the Germans had been negotiating a surrender in Italy for the past two months. He left the same day for Como, on the Swiss border, where he awaited a large force of Fascists with which he would make a last stand. Only a dozen arrived. Joined by Clara Petacci, he headed for the tunnel leading to the Austrian border, accompanied by a group of German soldiers.

The unit was stopped by partisans, who let the Germans through, but insisted on a thorough search of the trucks for Italians. Those they found they had driven to the nearby partisan headquarters at Dongo. Mussolini, faking a drunken slumber in a German overcoat and helmet, was one of those discovered. The plan was to hand him over to the partisans in Milan, but left-wing factions of the Committee, only too aware that their prize might be claimed by the Allies, demanded summary justice .

Colonel Valerio, the *nom de guerre* of an accountant, Walter Audisio, raced to Dongo on 28 April and forced the partisans there to hand Mussolini over to him. He rushed into the prisoner's room, crying 'I've come to liberate you!' He then drove Mussolini and Clara out of the town, stopped the car, and pulled out his gun, saying, 'I am instructed to do justice for the Italian people.' Mussolini's last words were 'Shoot me in the chest.'

The bodies of Mussolini and Clara Petacci were collected with the bodies of the other Fascists who had been rounded up and shot, and the next morning they were strung up by the heels from the frame of a half-built petrol station in Milan. The whole world saw the photographs of the ignominious end of Italy's Fascist leader. After his corpse was taken down, Benito Mussolini, Il Duce, was buried secretly in Milan. In 1957 the body was returned to his family and reburied in the cemetery in his home town.